STEP INTO NATURE

By the Roadside

Written by Michael Chinery
Illustrated by John Gosler

GRANADA

Published by Granada Publishing 1984
Granada Publishing Limited
8 Grafton Street, London W1X 3LA

Copyright © Templar Publishing Ltd 1984
Illustrations copyright © Templar Publishing Ltd 1984

British Library Cataloguing in Publication Data
Chinery, Michael
    By the roadside.– (Step into Nature; 6)
    1. Roadside fauna – Great Britain –
        Pictorial works – Juvenile literature
    2. Roadside flora – Great Britain –
        Pictorial works – Juvenile literature
    I. Title   II. Series
    574.5'264   QH137

    ISBN 0-246-12177-7

Series devised by Richard Carlisle
Edited by Mandy Wood
Designed by Mick McCarthy
Printed in Italy

Contents

At home in the hedgerow 4

The little brown wren 6

Nettles, dead or alive! 8

Birds among the branches .. 10

Hunters of the verge 12

Beetle battles 14

Climbing the hedge 16

The robin's pincushion 18

Two furry foragers 20

The great caterpillar hunt .. 22

The hedgerow calendar 24

The butterfly ball 26

Colourful shrubs 28

The crafty cuckoo 30

Silken snares 32

Flowers of lace 34

The life of a lichen 36

Roadside flowers 38

The thieving magpie 40

Picture index 42

No matter where you live, you are surrounded by nature. In the towns, even in the cities, you will find birds and animals, flowers and trees, bugs and grubs to watch and wonder about. STEP INTO NATURE is about all these things – the everyday creatures as well as the elusive. It's packed with nature projects to do, nature diaries to keep and clues and signs for the nature detective to read. It will teach you how to look at the world of nature around you, how to understand its working and how to conserve it for others.

At home in the hedgerow

No matter where you live, you can be sure that somewhere nearby there grows a hedge. See if you can find one locally – it will usually be made from a narrow strip of trees and shrubs and it may well be perched on a small bank. There will often be a ditch on one side of the hedge, and maybe a grassy verge between the hedge and the road. All these different regions are extremely important as homes for lots of different plants and animals. Many woodland creatures, for example, make their homes in our hedgerows when their original habitats are cut down. And plants and animals that once lived in the meadows often move to the roadside verges once the meadows have been ploughed up for growing crops. Water-loving creatures live in the ditch.

Some of the many plants and animals that you can find in and around the hedgerow appear in the picture below. How many can you recognise? They nearly all pop up again on later pages of this book. Take a walk along a local

① Magpie
② Ivy
③ Bank vole
④ Germander speedwell
⑤ Weasel
⑥ Stinging nettle
⑦ Hedge bindweed
⑧ Cowslip
⑨ Bramble
⑩ Dunnock
⑪ Cuckoo
⑫ Honeysuckle
⑬ Dandelion

4

hedgerow if you can and see how many different kinds of plants and animals you can find. Use your *Nature Diary* to record what you see. What kinds of shrubs make up the bulk of the hedge? How high do they grow? You can find the names of some of the common shrubs by looking at page 28 of this book.

Remember, though, that when studying nature by the roadside, you must always be very careful of the traffic. Never climb steep banks, for it is very easy to fall down into the road itself. It is much safer to explore the hedge from the side growing away from the road if you can, but get the land owner's permission first.

nature detective

How old is that hedge?

Many miles of hedge were planted in the 18th and 19th centuries, when Parliament decided that the ancient commons around the towns and villages should be enclosed for growing crops. These hedges were often planted entirely of hawthorn, because it grows very quickly, and they were usually quite straight. Many of our hedgerows are very much older than this, though, especially those along the roadsides. Some are the remains of woodlands that were left as boundaries or fences when the woods were cleared to make way for fields of crops and animals. Other old hedges simply sprang up on the no-man's land between neighbouring farms and villages. You can usually recognise these old hedges because they have large tree trunks or stumps in them and they are usually rather wavy – not straight like modern ones.

Perhaps you have a hedge near you that you think might be quite old. In fact, it's not too difficult to find out, thanks to a British biologist called Max Hooper. Dr Hooper studied a great many hedges and, by looking at old maps and documents, he was able to find out the ages of them fairly accurately. He then discovered that the number of different kinds of shrub growing in a hedge is closely linked to its age. He worked out a simple rule, and you can use it to work out how old your hedge is. Simply pace out a 30-metre stretch of hedgerow, avoiding corners and gateways, and count the number of different kinds of shrubs growing in that stretch (don't include climbers like the blackberry or wild rose, though). You can then say that the hedge is one hundred years old for each kind of shrub it contains. So one with six different shrubs will be 600 years old!

Guelder rose, a common hedgerow shrub.

The little brown wren

The wren is one of our smallest and shyest birds. It spends most of its time scampering about in the hedgerow or undergrowth, searching for food. In fact, it spends so much time scuffling about on the ground that many people mistake it for a mouse. But you'll soon see that it's a bird if you get a good look – its up-turned tail immediately identifies it. Notice also its slender beak which it uses like a pair of delicate tweezers to pick up tiny insects and spiders from among the leaf litter.

There is no mistaking the wren when it bursts into song. It has an incredibly loud voice for such a small bird, pouring out its high-pitched trills and whistles for quite long periods. You can hear this song at any time of year, but it is at its best and loudest in the spring when the male is defending his nesting territory.

During this spring period the male wren generally builds several domed nests of moss and leaves, but he never quite finishes them. Instead, he goes courting and persuades a female to visit his nests. If she likes the look of one of them, *she* will finish it off with a lining of feathers and other soft material before laying her eggs there. The male takes little notice of her after that, for he is busy searching for another female for one of his other nests! By the time spring is over, the father wren might end up with three wives and over 20 babies. But he is a good insect hunter and helps to feed them all. If you're lucky, you might even see a wren family hunting in the hedge and calling to each other with loud and rapid ticking sounds.

Wrens have great problems keeping their tiny bodies warm in winter and often huddle together in old nests or nest boxes at night. Many of them die in bad winters because they can't find enough food. Remember to put out food and water in your garden to help these and other birds.

nature watch

More small birds

The goldcrest and the firecrest seen on the right are Europe's smallest birds. Measuring only 9 cms from beak to tail, they are just a little smaller than the wren. Can you spot the difference between these two tiny birds? Look at the eyes. These are both males. The females are similar but they have yellow crests instead of orange. Look for these birds in hedgerows and along the edges of woods. The goldcrest is especially fond of coniferous trees. You will find it all over Europe. The firecrest only lives in southern and central Europe and in Britain you will find it only near the south coast. Listen for the high-pitched songs of these two birds – *tsee-tsee-tsee*, repeated time and time again. Look at their beaks. What kind of food do you think they eat?

Goldcrest

Firecrest

7

Nettles, dead or alive!

At first glance, you might think the plant in the big picture is a stinging nettle. But if you look closely you'll see its flowers are of quite a different type. In fact, this plant is a red *deadnettle* – so called because it has no sting and cannot attack us like the stinging nettle. Look for it on waste ground and also as a weed in your garden. If you find one, crush a piece of leaf and smell it. There are several different kinds of deadnettle and they nearly all have strong-smelling leaves. They belong to the mint family.

The deadnettle's tubular flowers are carried in whorls on the square-shaped stem, and hold lots of nectar. The bee approaching the flower in the picture is a potter bee. You will often see it on the deadnettles in spring, plunging its long tongue deep into the flowers to get at the nectar. It looks very much like a bumble bee, but it darts about much more rapidly. Look at the bee already feeding at the flowers. Can you see the large blob of pollen on its hind leg, ready to be taken back to the nest as food for its babies?

nature detective

Deadnettle look-alikes

Look out for these plants in hedgerows and on roadsides and waste ground. Their leaves are all carried in pairs and are often covered with soft hairs.

Hedge woundwort

(right) is like a tall red deadnettle with clear white blotches on its flowers. Look for it in shady hedgerows and also in the woods. Its leaves are rough to touch but they do not sting.

White dead-nettle *(left)* is extremely common. Feel its soft leaves: they don't sting. Can you smell their scent?

Henbit *(right)* is very like the red deadnettle but has more rounded leaves and its flowers are more slender.

The stinging nettle's sting

The stinging nettle can be thought of as the live nettle – the one that attacks you if you brush against it! The stings are produced by large hairs that are scattered over its leaves and stems. Put on some gloves and then pick a small piece of nettle. Have a good look at it with a magnifying glass. Can you see some large hairs like the ones in the drawing below? They look like miniature bottles with long necks. These are the stings. When you brush against a nettle you break off the very delicate glass-like bead at the tip of the hair, leaving the needle-like point exposed. Any further pushing against the plant makes the point stick into you and poison flows up from the bottle and into your body. It isn't really dangerous but it can make you sore for a few hours. The stings are actually there to protect the plant from grazing animals. Rabbits, for example, don't like stinging nettles, and you can often see the plants growing around the rabbits' burrows where few others can survive. Stinging nettles really enjoy disturbed ground: you can find them almost anywhere that the ground has been dug up, and especially where people have dumped rubbish. You probably don't like stinging nettles, but they do have their uses. The caterpillars of some of our prettiest butterflies eat them!

The stinging nettle carries its tiny green flowers in catkins.

The stinging hairs, greatly magnified.

Self-Heal (above) grows on grassy roadsides. Its leaves are downy but have no scent.

Yellow archangel (right) has a strong smell. Look for it in damp hedgerows and woods.

Birds among the branches

Keep your eyes and ears open as you walk along the roadside and you'll probably be amazed at the number of birds you can find, even in a town. Some are easy to spot, while others prefer to stay hidden in the middle of the hedge. You can usually tell they're there, though, by listening for their calls. Be patient and look carefully, but never pull the branches about when you're searching for birds.

You will frighten them and might even damage their nests if you do this.

Use your *Nature Diary* to record when and where you find different birds. If they are feeding, try to find out what they are actually eating. Some of the common hedgerow birds are pictured here, but there are many others such as the song thrush and the blackbird. What other birds do you often see in hedges?

The **turtle dove** is a summer visitor to Europe, arriving from Africa around the end of April. It commonly nests in thick hedges and often feeds on the roadside verge. If disturbed, it will fly up to reveal its black tail, prominently bordered with white. You might see small flocks of these birds in the summer.

The **greenfinch** likes thick hedges and dense undergrowth. You can find it in town parks and churchyards as well as in the country, often in flocks of ten or more. It feeds almost entirely on seeds and is very fond of peanuts (the unsalted variety). The bird here is a male; the female is less colourful.

The **goldfinch** is usually seen in small groups known as *charms*. It is very common on the roadsides, where it feeds on a wide variety of seeds. It doesn't always wait for them to ripen, though, and can often be seen pulling the flowers of dandelions and thistles to pieces to get at the soft young seeds.

The **dunnock**, also called the hedge sparrow, is a rather shy bird usually found in dense bushes and hedgerows. You can often see it in town parks and gardens. Notice the grey neck and breast and the slender beak, which immediately separate this bird from the house sparrow. It usually feeds on the ground.

Bullfinches usually go about in pairs. You will probably see the brightly coloured male first, but his mate will not normally be far away. The bullfinch's favourite foods in spring are the buds and flowers of hawthorn. However, it also raids orchards and gardens and eats huge numbers of buds there, too.

The **chaffinch** is one of our commonest birds. You can find it wherever there are trees and bushes. Look for the white shoulder stripe and wing bars. The brownish female has these as well as the colourful male. Like the other finches, the chaffinch feeds mainly on seeds. Notice its stout beak.

Most owls come out at night, but you can often see the **little owl** in the daytime. Look for it sitting on a fence post or in a hedgerow tree, watching for its prey. It may bob its head up and down if you get too close, and then fly off. Listen for its cry of *kee-oo, kee-oo* and watch its rising and falling movement during flight.

The **long-tailed tit** can be found in thick hedgerows and along woodland margins, often in large family groups. The birds scour the twigs and branches for insects and call continuously to each other with squeaky *see-see-see* sounds. They build cosy nests of moss and feathers and even put roofs on them!

The **whitethroat** is a summer visitor to Europe. Can you see how it got its name? This is the male bird: the female has a brown head instead of grey. Look for the whitethroat in thick hedges, and listen for its *wit-wit-wit* call as it flies along or perches on its favourite branch.

The **sedge warbler** usually lives in damp areas, nesting in bushes and hedges close to ponds and streams as well as in reed beds. Look for the broad white stripe over the eye to identify this summer visitor to Europe. Notice the slender beak. What do you think this bird eats?

11

Hunters of the verge

Have you ever been travelling along a country road and seen a slender brown animal shoot across in front of you? If so, it was probably a stoat or a weasel. These quick-footed animals are quite common in hedgerows and on grassy verges. You can see both of them in the picture – the animal on the left, carrying one of its babies, is a stoat. The other is a weasel. Stoats are quite a lot bigger than weasels, but can you see any other differences?

Both animals can run surprisingly fast on their short legs, and they are both fierce predators. They rely mainly on scent to find their prey when stalking through the long grass of the verge, and hunt by night as well as day. Rabbits are the stoat's favourite prey, but it catches many other animals as well. An agile climber, it often climbs up to bird's nests to eat the eggs or young birds. The stoat is not easy to watch because it likes to keep to thick cover, but if you see one streak into the hedge it is worth keeping very still and making soft squeaking noises. The stoat is a rather inquisitive animal and may come out to see what is going on. You may even be lucky enough to see a whole family, for the youngsters often hunt with their mother in the autumn. The stoat is a very good mother, and if she thinks her nest is in danger she will carry her babies to a safer place. In many northern areas the stoat turns white for the winter. Why do you think this happens?

The weasel behaves in much the same way as the stoat except that it often stands up on its back legs to have a look around. And, because of its smaller size, it usually takes smaller prey – mice and voles being its favourites. It is slim enough to be able to enter their burrows to catch them.

nature detective

Stoat look-alikes

On the right you can see three of the stoat's relatives. They are the same shape as the stoat but all of them are a little larger and their colours make it easy for you to tell them apart.

The **mink** is an American animal which was brought to Europe to be bred for its fur. However, many mink escaped and can now be found living wild in parts of Britain and northern Europe. They live mainly by rivers, catching fish and other animals. There is also a European mink which lives mainly in eastern Europe. It has white on the top of its snout as well as the bottom.

The **polecat** lives in most parts of Europe, but if you want to see it in Britain you will have to go to Wales or its neighbouring counties in England. It feeds on rabbits and many other animals. The **ferret** is a domestic form of the polecat which people keep for catching rabbits. Try to find out how ferrets are used. Many of them are white or very pale brown, but others are rich brown and some look just like polecats.

Ferret
30-45cms long (without tail)

Polecat
30-45cms long (without tail)

American mink
35-40cms long (without tail)

Beetle battles

The two beetles in the big picture are male stag beetles. They get their name because of their great "antlers". But, unlike those belonging to deer, the stag beetle's antlers are really overgrown jaws. They might look quite frightening, but despite this they can't actually hurt you. The antlers can't be used for biting – the beetles use them for wrestling instead!

The two beetles in the picture are not really trying to hurt each other. Their battle is simply a trial of strength, with each one trying to impress a female who is probably watching nearby. The fight may go on for half an hour or more, but one beetle will eventually get tired and slink away, leaving the stronger one to claim the female. She is a little smaller than the male and has no antlers.

After mating, the female lays her eggs in dead and decaying tree trunks and stumps, especially those of oaks. The fat white grubs feed on the rotten wood for three years before turning into new beetles. Try looking for adults in May or June, especially in the evenings. They are not as common as they used to be because we don't have so many oak woods now, but they still occur in many places. Parks with old trees, even in the middle of towns, are quite good places to look for them. And so are country lanes, especially those with thick hedges. The hedges often contain old tree stumps or thick old fence posts in which the beetles can breed. If you're lucky you might see one of them flying through the air with a great buzzing of wings, or even come across two males having a fight!

The male stag beetle is about 5 cms long, including its antlers, which is pretty big for a beetle. But some of its tropical relatives are over three times as big – the Hercules beetle of America, for instance, is 18 cms long, although more than half of this is accounted for by its huge horns.

nature detective

More big beetles

Keep your eyes and ears open for other large beetles in the hedgerows. Most of them start to fly around at dusk, and many make quite a noise with their wings as they zoom along. By day you can find them on the vegetation.

The **cockchafer** (left), often called the maybug, flies in May and June. It is about 2.5 cms long. It damages forests by nibbling young shoots, and its grub destroys cereal roots in the soil.

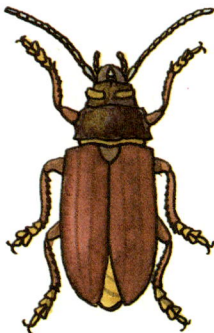

The **tanner beetle** (left) grows up to 4 cms long. It belongs to a group known as longhorn beetles – if you look at its antennae you'll probably see why. Its grub feeds in decaying stumps. You can sometimes find the beetle on hogweed flowers.

Cerambyx cerdo (right) does not occur in Britain and has no English name. It is one of the largest European beetles, growing to about 5 cms long. Like the tanner beetle, it is a longhorn. Look for it in wooded areas in most parts of Europe.

14

Climbing the hedge

All green plants need sunlight to help them grow, and those of the hedgerow are no exception. They struggle against each other in the race to grow big and strong, and the tallest plants usually win by keeping the sunlight from their shorter relatives. Some plants, however, have managed to succeed without producing big strong stems. They merely climb up their neighbours instead. See how many of these climbing plants you can find in the hedgerows. Some of them are shown in the big picture.

Many of these climbers have their very own method of creeping up the hedge. The stems and leaves of the cleavers or goosegrass, for instance, are clothed with minute hooks which catch in the leaves of other plants and hold the cleavers up. Hedge bindweed, on the other hand, actually coils itself around its neighbours, always in an anti-clockwise direction. The plant dies down in the autumn, but its underground parts send soft new shoots spiralling up the hedge in the spring. Bittersweet, also known as woody nightshade, is another climber which scrambles over plants by twining around them in any way it can. You might also see brambles and wild roses climbing up the hedge-row, using their curved prickles to hook onto other plants. (You can read more about the wild rose on page 18.)

Finally, have a look at the ivy stems climbing on trees and walls. Can you see the tiny roots sprouting from the stems? They push themselves into small cracks in the surface beneath them and so hold the ivy up. Notice how the shape of the leaves changes from being star-like at the bottom of the hedge to heart-shaped near the top, where they are in full light.

Bittersweet

Bramble

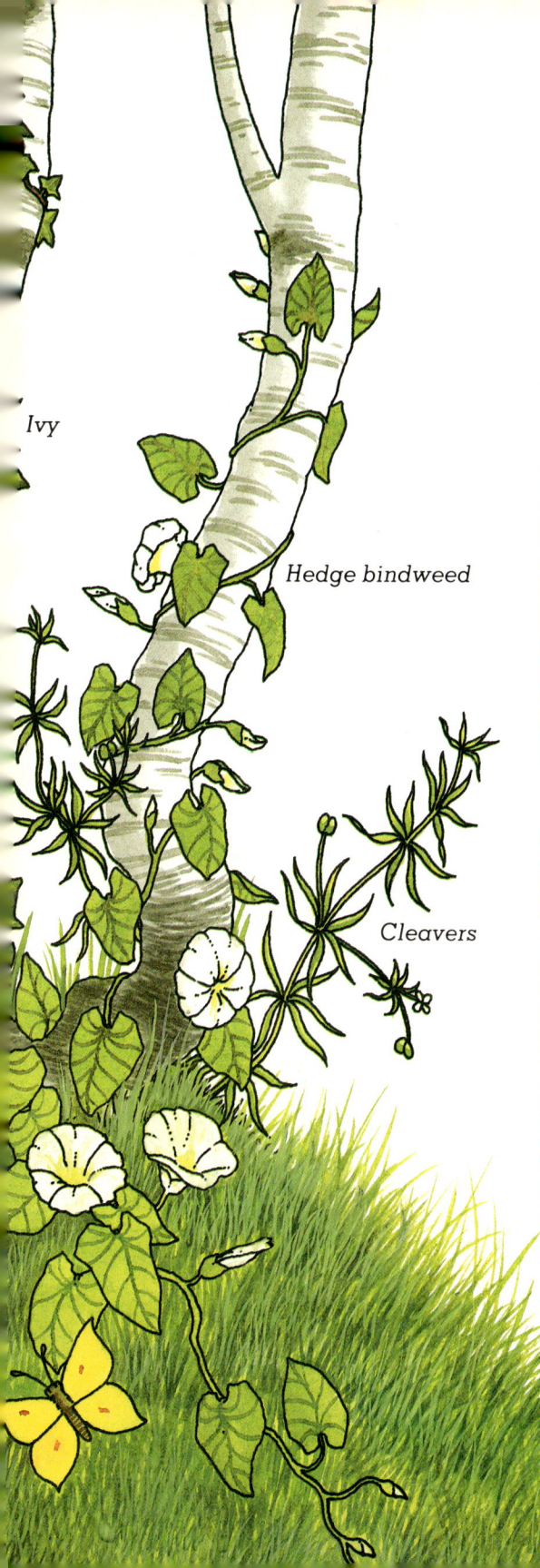

Ivy

Hedge bindweed

Cleavers

The ivy's feast

Huge numbers of insects come to drink sweet nectar from the ivy flowers in the autumn. By day numerous flies, such as the greenbottle below, visit the flowers, together with queen wasps who fill up with food in preparation for their long winter sleep. At night these insects are replaced by many different moths who also come to feast from the flowers. Choose a patch of blossom in October and watch it for 15 minutes to see how many insects come to drink. Can you see the beads of nectar for yourself?

Clinging cleavers

You have probably stuck the little fruits or burrs of the cleavers on your friends' clothes or had them stuck on you! But have you ever wondered just why they stick? Next time you find some of the little burrs have a good look at them with a magnifying glass. You will see that they are covered with hundreds of tiny hooks. How do you think this helps the plant to reproduce?

17

The robin's pincushion

The beautiful flower in the picture is a wild rose. Notice its hooked prickles which help it to climb over its neighbours in the hedge. Keep your eyes open and you'll probably see this rose flowering along the roadside in the summer. And later on in the year its bright red fruits, known as hips, again brighten the hedge with their own colourful display. But apart from being quite lovely to look at, the wild rose provides food and shelter for many hedgerow creatures. Bees and other insects collect pollen from its flowers, while its fruits are eagerly gobbled up by hungry birds in the winter. What's more, if you explore the plant thoroughly you may find yet another visitor who has made the rose its home.

Almost certainly you will find some hairy red or orange balls on the rose stems. These strange growths are known as robin's pincushions, although they don't have any connection with robins apart from their colour. They grow on the leaves and stems of the rose through the action of some tiny insects called gall wasps. In scientific language, the pincushion is a gall. There are many different kinds of gall, each one caused by a different insect or other animal.

The story of the pincushion gall begins in the spring, when the rose buds begin to open. The gall wasps lay their eggs in the buds and soon the little grubs hatch out and start to nibble the plant tissues. This irritates the rose, which gradually swells up around the grubs to form the gall. The grubs don't mind this at all, for the gall is full of good plant material for them to eat. Each grub has its own little chamber, where it feeds until it's fully grown. Then it turns into a new wasp and emerges in spring to lay more eggs on more roses!

18

Gather the galls

By gathering a few galls you can rear the insects from them and then watch the new galls grow.

1 Collect the galls between autumn and early spring. Put them in a jar and keep them cool during the winter.

2 The gall wasps *(left)* will leave the galls in the spring. How many emerge from a single gall? Put a few of them in a small muslin or nylon bag.

3 Fix the bag around a rose twig and your gall wasps may lay eggs in the buds. You can then watch the new galls grow. How many are there?

The rose's other guests

Look for these other insects on wild or garden roses. You will usually notice the damage they do before you see the insects.

The **leaf-cutter bee** *(left)* cuts neat semicircles from rose leaves and carries them away to use for building its nest.

Pale patches on leaves are the work of the **rose-slug** *(right)* – an insect grub which strips the leaf surface.

Two furry foragers

Look carefully at the two mouse-like animals in the picture. Can you see any differences between them apart from their colour? Look at the shape of their heads and snouts. What about the ears? If you look closely you'll see they are, in fact, two very different animals. The one at the top is a shrew and the other is a bank vole. They are not mice. Try to find a picture of a mouse to compare with them.

The shrew belongs to the group of animals called *insectivores*. This name means insect-eaters, but the shrew actually eats all kinds of small animals, including slugs and worms. It sniffs them out with its long, sensitive snout and then uses its big front teeth to pick them up. Stop and listen carefully when you are walking by the hedgerow. You might well hear the high pitched squeaks of the shrews as they hunt for food in the dead leaves and grass at the bottom of the hedge. You'll be very lucky if you actually see one of them, though, for they are quite tiny animals – with bodies only about 8 cms long. Despite this, they need a surprising amount of food to keep themselves warm, and spend nearly all day and night hunting for tasty morsels to eat, taking just short naps every now and then.

The bank vole at the bottom of the picture belongs to the group of gnawing animals that we called *rodents* – the same group that contains the mice and squirrels. It eats some small animals, but feeds mainly on fruits, seeds and other vegetable matter. Like the shrew, it is active by day and by night, but you are more likely to see this creature because it often climbs bushes to nibble the fruits. The one in the picture is feasting on blackberries. Hazel nuts are another of its favourite foods. It nibbles a neat round hole in the shell to get at the kernel.

Teeth for the job

nature watch

An animal's teeth are its main tools and, just as a carpenter has different tools for different jobs, so animals have different teeth for different foods! Look at the picture below and you will see that the teeth of the vole are quite unlike those of the shrew. The vole is largely vegetarian and uses its very sharp, chisel-like front teeth to gnaw through hard nuts and tough grass stems. It then uses the flat grinding teeth at the back of its mouth to crush the food before it is swallowed. The shrew, on the other hand, feeds on small animals and uses its pointed teeth to hold them securely so they can't escape. The sharp edges also slice up the flesh. Try to find some jaws and teeth to see this for yourself. One place to look is in an owl pellet. Pull one apart and you will probably find some inside.

Vole

Shrew

The great caterpillar hunt

In the summer just one short stretch of hedgerow can provide a home for thousands of leaf-eating caterpillars. See if you can find some of these interesting creatures to study yourself. They are not always easy to spot because many of them are beautifully camouflaged to blend in with their leafy surroundings. And others can look just like the twigs on which they sit if they keep still! However, even if you can't see the caterpillars themselves to start with, you can often track them down by looking for tell-tale signs or clues. Bare twigs on a leafy bush, for example, might show you where some caterpillars have been feeding. Look out also for partly chewed leaves and for droppings scattered on the leaves at the bottom of the hedge.

Many caterpillars are active mainly at night, so it's a good idea to have a look at your hedge with a torch just after dark. Look on nettles and other low-growing plants as well as on the hedgerow shrubs. You may find butterfly caterpillars on the grasses and other low-growing plants, but those larvae feeding on the shrubs will nearly always grow into moths.

Five common hedgerow caterpillars, all belonging to moths, are pictured

① Privet hawkmoth caterpillar: up to 10cms
② Garden tiger moth caterpillar: up to 6cms
③ Magpie moth caterpillar: up to 3cms
④ Grey dagger moth caterpillar: up to 4cms
⑤ Bufftip moth caterpillar: up to 5cms

22

below. You can see that some of them are patterned to help hide them from hungry birds while others, such as the magpie moth caterpillar, are very brightly coloured. These gaudy caterpillars don't have to hide from their enemies because they are very unpleasant to eat and their colours warn birds of this fact.

The magpie caterpillar is one of a group called *loopers*: see how it moves by arching its body in a large loop. It grips the twig beneath very tightly with its two pairs of hind legs. If you could look at these legs under a microscope you would see that they are covered with hundreds of minute hooks which provide the grip. Most other caterpillars have five pairs of fleshy legs near the back instead of two.

Keeping caterpillars

It is easy to keep caterpillars at home and watch them grow up and turn into butterflies or moths. You must make sure that they have regular supplies of the right kind of leaves to eat.

And remember not to handle them unnecessarily. When the caterpillars are fully grown they will turn into chrysalises or pupae. Some pupate on the twigs of their food plant but others prefer to pupate in the soil. So put some peat and moss in the cage.

1 You can make a simple caterpillar cage from a biscuit tin and some clear plastic sheet. Put some twigs of the right food plant in a jar of water and plug the top with tissue before you put it in the cage. Change tho twigs regularly.

2 Your caterpillars will change their skins several times as they grow. They stay very still for a couple of days while doing this. Never touch them. When fully grown, some spin a cocoon like that on the left and turn into a chrysalis inside it. The one in our drawing belongs to an emperor moth.

3 When the adult moth or butterfly comes out of its chrysalis its wings will be all crumpled. It will need plenty of room to stretch and harden its wings before it can fly away. Let it go when it is ready.

⑤

The hedgerow calendar

Winter

In winter you can see the bare, dark twigs of the hedgerow shrubs, often being buffeted by the cold wind. This is a good time to examine the sharp thorns that make the blackthorn and hawthorn such good barriers, for few animals can get through them. You might also spot flocks of fieldfares searching for the last of the hedgerow fruits, but a few rose-hips is all they'll find. Meanwhile the colourful robin sings from his perch on the bramble.

Spring

In spring the hedgerow bursts into life. The blackthorn bushes are covered with snowy white flowers even before their leaves open. And the strong-smelling blossoms of the hawthorn follow early in May. Lesser celandines, violets and white deadnettle flower in the hedge bottom while rabbits graze on the young grass and dandelions. Blackbirds busily collect materials to make their nests, and butterflies, like the small tortoiseshell, bask in the spring sunshine.

Unless it is full of evergreens, such as holly or yew, the hedgerow alters dramatically from season to season – often with startling changes of colour. Use your *Nature Diary* to record what you see in the hedgerow at different times of the year.

Summer

Summer sees the hedgerow alive with activity of all kinds. You might see families of birds, like the blue tit, searching for insects in the hedgerow, while colourful butterflies like the brimstone sip nectar from the flowers. Climbing plants such as the honeysuckle, wild rose, bramble and bindweed drape their beautiful flowers over the hedge, while knapweed, hogweed and plantain flower abundantly on the verge below.

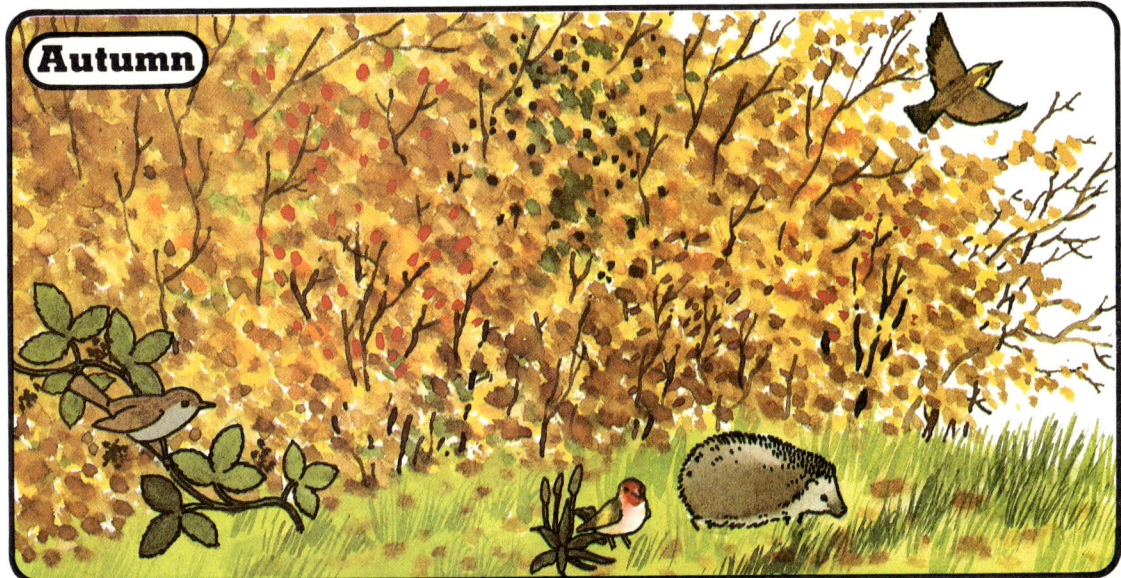

Autumn

Autumn is the time for fruit. Look for blackberries and the poisonous fruits of bryony and bittersweet, as well as a new crop of rose-hips. The hedgerow birds all have a feast – goldfinches stuff themselves with plantain seeds on the verge, while the yellowhammer and dunnock hunt for seeds in the hedge. The hedgehog also fills himself up before his long winter sleep. Notice the changing colours of the leaves before they fall and it becomes winter again.

The butterfly ball

The roadside is a very good place for watching butterflies because lots of different flowers grow in the hedges and along the verge. The flowers themselves provide nectar for the adult insects, while their leaves are eagerly nibbled by caterpillars. How many kinds of butterflies can you find in your local hedgerow? Some of the commoner ones are pictured here. Use your *Nature Diary* to record when and where you see them and on which flowers.

① The **comma butterfly** gets its name because of the white mark on its underside. It sleeps in the hedge all through the winter, its ragged wings making it look just like a dead leaf.

② The **map butterfly** does not live in Britain, although it is very common on the continent. Those that hatch in the

Male

④

Female

①

②

③

26

spring have a very different wing pattern from those that emerge in summer.

3 The **brimstone** also sleeps through the winter, usually in holly and ivy bushes. With its wings folded, it looks like a pale green leaf. It wakes very early in spring.

4 The pretty **holly blue** can often be seen flitting along the hedgerow. Its caterpillars feed on the flower buds and young berries of both holly and ivy.

5 The **hedge brown** is a familiar hedgerow butterfly in England and Wales. It is also called the gatekeeper, because it likes to bask in sunny gateways along the hedgerows. It is particularly fond of bramble blossom.

6 The **orange-tip butterfly** can be seen feeding on garlic mustard and cuckoo-flower. Its slender green caterpillars also feed on these plants.

7 The **ringlet** can usually be found on bramble blossom, along with the hedge brown. You can recognise it by the ringed eye-spots on its underside. The upper side is dark brown.

All the butterflies on this page are drawn at about their right size, except for the hedge brown and the map butterfly which are about twice their natural size.

Female

Male

7

Female

Male

5

6

Colourful shrubs

How many different kinds of shrub can you find in your local hedgerows? By counting them up you may even be able to tell how long the hedges have been growing there (see page 5).

One shrub you are almost bound to come across is the hawthorn. It's one of our commonest hedgerow shrubs, growing very quickly and often forming whole hedges. Don't confuse it with the blackthorn, though, which is another very spiky hedgerow shrub. English elm was also once very widely planted in hedgerows. The large trees were used for timber, while the suckers springing from their roots made good thick boundary hedges. The snowberry also sends up lots of suckers in this way.

Many hedgerow shrubs have brightly coloured berries. They provide food for lots of different creatures, but never eat any yourself because many of them are poisonous. You can see some common shrubs and their fruits on this page.

Blackthorn bushes are clothed with snowy white flowers in early spring, long before the leaves appear. The fruits are called sloes and are like small but very bitter plums.

The strong-smelling flowers of **elder** are at their best in May and June. Both the flowers and fruits of this bush are used for making wine.

Dogwood produces domed heads of creamy flowers in early summer and black fruits in autumn. Look for the reddish stems which identify this shrub at all times of the year.

The **wayfaring tree** grows on lime-rich soils. Its wrinkled leaves are rather furry underneath. The fruits, which are black when ripe, are flattened from side to side.

The **pussy willow** has two sorts of catkins which appear before the leaves. The golden, pollen-carrying ones are males and grow on different trees from the silvery female ones.

Hawthorn is often called the may, because it flowers at the beginning of this month. The fruits are called haws. Notice the sharp thorns which help to make this shrub a good barrier.

Wild privet grows on chalky soils. Its flowers have a very strong, sweet smell and it keeps some of its leaves in winter. Cultivated forms are planted for garden hedges.

Spindle has square-shaped twigs. The berries are especially attractive when they split to reveal the orange-coated seeds towards the middle of autumn.

Snowberry was introduced from North America. It forms dense clumps and its round white fruits are very noticeable when the leaves fall in autumn.

The **English elm** has very rough leaves. The flowers come out before the leaves and produce bunches of circular, winged fruits in early summer.

The crafty cuckoo

Every year in April and May the well-known cry of the cuckoo rings through the woods and hedgerows. Listen out for the loud *cook-coo* call from which the bird gets its name.

The cuckoo is rather a lazy bird and doesn't make a nest for its eggs like other birds. Instead, the female spends a lot of time sitting in the trees and hedgerows just watching the other birds build theirs! She waits patiently for them to lay their eggs and then, when a nest is unattended, she sneaks in to make a crafty swap! She lays one of her own eggs in the nest and removes one of the originals, usually by eating it, to keep the numbers right. As long as there are enough suitable nests in the area, the cuckoo will lay up to 20 eggs, all in different places, in five or six weeks. You can see the crafty mother cuckoo sitting on a branch to the right of the big picture.

The cuckoo uses several different small birds to act as foster parents for its babies. They include robins, meadow pipits, pied wagtails, sedge warblers and dunnocks. Each female cuckoo normally sticks to just one kind, however, and her eggs are usually quite a good match for those already in the nest. The foster parents don't seem too bothered that the

cuckoo's egg is quite a lot bigger than their own. Nor by the fact that when the cuckoo hatches the first thing that it does is to throw all the other eggs or nestlings out of the nest! It needs a lot of food, and getting rid of the others ensures that the young cuckoo gets everything that its foster parents bring along.

The baby soon outgrows both its foster parents and their tiny nest, but as long as it keeps opening its beak for food, they will carry on feeding it. It eventually leaves the nest when it's about three weeks old, but the foster parents continue to give it food for another two. By this time it really dwarfs them! You can see that the baby cuckoo in the picture is so big that the poor little dunnock is having to perch on its back to feed it.

nature match

Look for the cuckoo

The cuckoo is a summer visitor to Europe, usually arriving from Africa in April. Listen out for the male's familiar call and note down the date when you first hear it in your *Nature Diary*. The male usually sings from the trees, especially at the edges of woods. See if you can track him down by listening for his song. The female's call is less often heard. It sounds rather like water being poured from a bottle! Look for the female flying low over fields and hedgerows. She has long, pointed wings and a rounded tail.

nature detective

A cuckoo's hairy dinner

Cuckoos are among the few birds that eat *hairy* cater-pillars. The hairs stick in the mouths and throats of most birds and irritate them, but the cuckoo doesn't seem to mind. Look for some of these hairy caterpillars yourself. Hawthorn hedges make good hunting grounds. Two common caterpillars are shown here. Don't handle them, though, or the hairs might irritate your skin.

Gold-tail moth caterpillar

Vapourer moth caterpillar

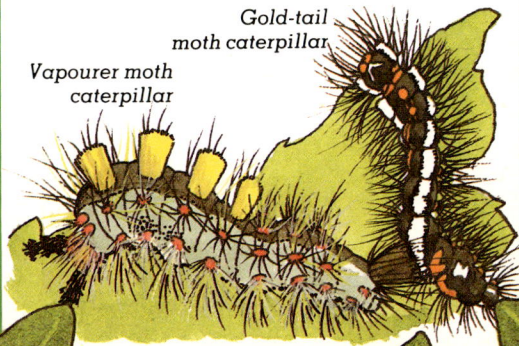

Silken snares

Many people think that spiders are insects, but they are really a quite different sort of creature. They belong to a group known as *arachnids* and whereas insects have only three pairs of legs, arachnids always have four. The colourful spider in the picture is called *Argiope*. It is common in many parts of Europe, but in England you'll only find it in counties along the south coast.

Argiope belongs to a large group known as the orb-web spiders. And although *Argiope* itself is rare in Britain many of its relatives are very common. They all spin wheel-shaped webs on hedges and fences. See how many of these webs you can spot by the roadside. Look out also for the garden spider – a plump brown creature with white dots forming a cross on its back.

People often think that spiders spin webs only in the autumn, but you can find orb-webs in the spring and summer as well. They are more obvious in the autumn simply because the spiders are larger then and their webs are bigger. The webs are also often decorated with dew and frost at this time of year which helps to make them more noticeable. The webs are, of course, really intended as insect traps. They are made of sticky silk produced from within the spiders' bodies. And when insects fly into them they are held there by the silk, giving the spider a chance to bite them with its poisonous fangs. Once its victims are well and truly caught, the spider may wrap them up with more silk before sucking out their juices. Do remember, though, that although spiders have poisonous fangs, no British species is dangerous to human beings, so they are really *not* creatures to be frightened of.

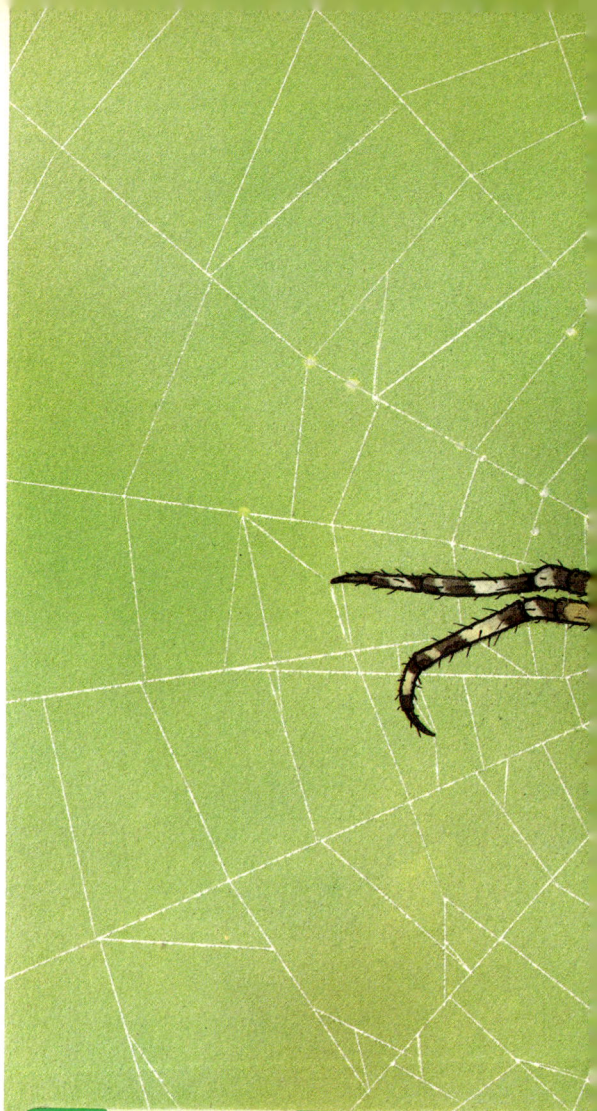

nature detective

An assortment of webs

The wheel-shaped orb-web is just one of many designs used by spiders. How many other kinds can you find on walls and hedgerows? Two common forms are shown on the right. The star-shaped web at the bottom belongs to a spider called *Segestria*. This spider usually lives in cracks in walls and rushes out to catch any insect that trips over one of the silken threads. Try tickling the web with a piece of grass and see what happens. You will find lots of other lacy webs sprouting from cracks in the wall.

Weavers at work

The spider has to re-build its web quite often because it is easily damaged. If you search the hedgerows carefully in the morning you might see the re-building taking place. The outer framework, attached to surrounding twigs, is re-used if it is safe enough.

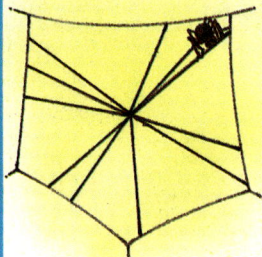

1 When the outer framework is complete the spider makes numerous radii, rather like the spokes of a wheel. Large webs have more radii than small webs. Try to count the radii in several webs.

2 When all the radii are in place the spider spins a loose spiral of non-sticky threads, starting from the centre of the web. She is then ready to begin the final stage of her deadly trap.

3 When laying down the sticky threads the spider starts from the outside. Watch how she draws the silk from her hind end with her legs and then sticks it neatly to the radii – always at exactly the right spot. How long does the spider take to make the web?

The hammock web (*above*) is very common in bushes and hedgerows. Look for the tiny spider hanging underneath the web. It catches insects which bump into the threads and fall on the sheet.

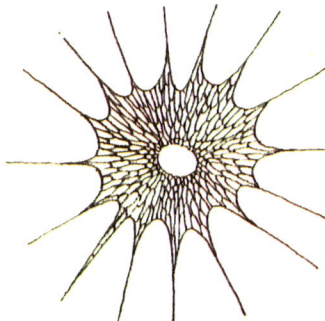

Flowers of lace

Walk along almost any hedgerow or roadside verge in the summer and you will see beautiful, umbrella-like flower-heads, similar to the one in the picture. They belong to the hogweed or keck and grow to a height of about 1.5 metres. Try to find such a plant and look carefully at the flower-heads. You will see that they are made up of hundreds of tiny white or pink flowers, spread out like a lacy table mat. In fact, one of the hogweed's close relatives is sometimes called Queen Anne's lace, although we know it better as cow parsley. You can find it in flower in late spring. Look out also for the giant hogweed, an invader from Asia which can reach heights of 5 metres.

Notice how all the hogweed's flower stalks fan out from one point. Each small flower has five petals, but the petals are not all the same size. Can you see that the flowers on the outside of each head are larger than those nearer the middle. The showy flower-heads, known as umbels, make splendid dinner tables for many flies and other insects. Most of them are eager to lap up the sugary nectar which the flowers produce. Look at the flowers with a magnifying glass and you might well see the glistening droplets of nectar lying there – as long as the insects haven't taken them already!

The hogweed belongs to the same family as the carrot and parsnip. There are also many popular herbs, such as parsley, in this large family. All have umbrella-like flower-heads and their leaves are often finely divided. The cook must be very careful when gathering them, though, because there are also many very poisonous plants in the family. You can see some of these in the panel on the right.

nature watch

Eaters eaten

Keep a watch on a patch of hogweed or a similar flower for a while and note down what the different insect visitors are doing. Watch the hover-flies dabbing their spongy tongues on the flowers to mop up the nectar. You might also notice that not all the visitors to these lacy dining tables are there to lap up the nectar. Some come to capture other insects instead. You might see a soldier beetle grab a small fly, for instance, or even a dance-fly like the one on the right stab another fly with its long beak and carry it away to suck out its juices.

The hogweed's family

How many different kinds of plant can you find with flower-heads like the hogweed? There are lots of them by the roadside. Some have white flowers, others are yellow. The shape of the fruit often helps to identify the plants. Remember that some are poisonous.

Cow parsley *(right)* is very common in the hedge and flowers in late spring. It has a rather strong smell and egg-shaped black fruits.

Alexander's *(left)* grows on waste ground and hedgebanks, especially near the sea. It has glossy green leaves divided into broad leaflets. The flowers are tightly packed in domed heads and the fruits are shiny black.

Hemlock *(right)* is a very poisonous plant with purple spots and streaks on its stem. It has ferny leaves and grows mainly in damp places. The fruit is rounded, with wavy ridges.

Fool's parsley *(left)* is extremely poisonous. It often grows in gardens, where its shiny green leaves could be mistaken for real parsley. When in flower, you can always recognise it by the "beards" under the flowers.

The life of a lichen

Take a look at some old walls. You will probably find that most of them are covered with patches of colour, almost as if they have been splashed with paint. The splashes may be white or greyish green, or even bright orange, and they are made by some flowerless plants called lichens. The orange one in the picture is called *Xanthoria*. Look at it closely and you will see that it is made up of spreading branches. The patches usually grow in circles but often there are so many of them growing in one place that they join into a shapeless mass.

Lichens are extremely hardy plants. They can survive on dry rocks and walls in the full sun, where they get very hot, and on rocks and stones high up in the mountains where they get very cold. Lichens grow very slowly indeed, with the circular patches often creeping outwards at no more than 1mm per year. However, the colonies live on for a very long time, growing steadily by a small amount each year. So biologists can actually use the sizes of lichen patches to find out the approximate ages of old buildings and monuments. Visit your local churchyard and look at the lichens growing on the grave-stones. You will find dates on the stones. Are the biggest lichens always on the oldest stones? Look for lichens on tree trunks as well; they often look like miniature bushes.

Several small animals browse on the lichens, like the millipede at the top of the picture, while the zebra spider often hides there to do its hunting. The wall butterfly is not interested in the lichens, but likes to sunbathe on sunny walls. Make notes in your *Nature Diary* of the other creatures you find on lichen-covered walls.

nature detective

Looking for lichens

Not all lichens are as colourful as the *Xanthoria* in the big picture so you can easily miss them growing on rocks and tree trunks. But if you really pay attention and look carefully you will see that lichens grow almost everywhere. Only in the middle of large towns and by really busy roads will you find lichens missing from the trees and walls and rocks. Can you think why the lichens don't grow beside busy roads? Look at a few large lorries for a clue. Lichens are not all easy to identify, but you should be able to pick out those on the right when you see them.

How clean is your town?

Lichens are very hardy but they can't stand smoke and other forms of air pollution. So the number of lichens growing on walls and trees is a measure of the cleanness of the air. How many lichens can you find on a short stretch of wall in the centre of town? Look at similar stretches of wall further from the centre. Are there more lichens on these walls? If so, it means that the air gets cleaner as you get further from the middle.

The lichen below is *Lecanora muralis*, one of the commonest town lichens. It tolerates smoke better than most other species. Look for it on concrete and asbestos buildings as well as on gravestones. How big are the patches?

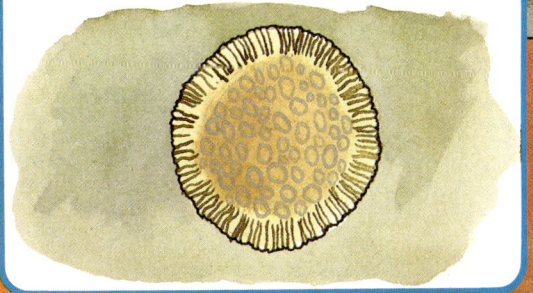

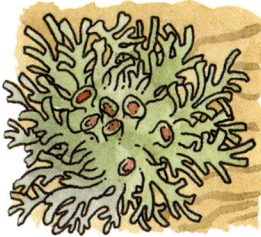

Hypogymnia physodes *(left)* clings very tightly to rocks, walls and tree trunks. The cleaner the air, the higher up this lichen will grow. Tiny spores grow in the coloured patches in the centre.

Tree-lungwort *(right)* is a leaf-like lichen which grows on tree trunks. It needs very clean air and in Britain you will find it only in the north and west – in woods as well as on roadside trees.

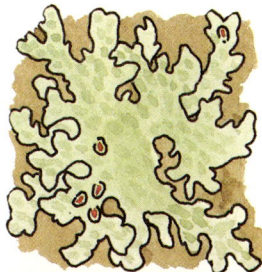

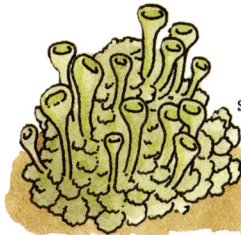

Pixie-cup lichens *(left)* grow on the ground and on tree stumps and trunks. The "cups" are covered with fine powder which flakes off and grows into new plants.

Ochrolechia parella *(right)* grows like a hard crust on rocks and walls and has a very prominent white border. The spore cups are like minute jam tarts.

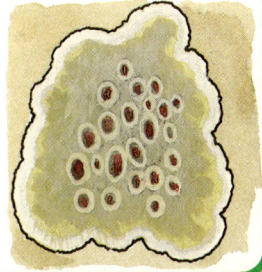

Roadside flowers

You can find plants in flower along the roadside at almost any time of the year. They soon spring up on waste ground or on bare earth left by roadworks, and brighten the verge with their colourful display. You can often find the plants of the grass verge growing in meadows as well, while those that thrive in the shade of the hedge are commonly found in woodland. Have a look in your garden, too. The plants of the hedgerow often occur in the flower beds as weeds!

1 Wild snapdragon is a relative of our garden snapdragons. It flowers all the summer. Watch the bumblebees force their way in between the petals to reach the nectar and pollen. The flower is sometimes yellow.

2 Ivy-leaved toadflax sprawls over walls and rocky banks and flowers from spring to autumn.

3 Germander speedwell is one of several similar plants. The flowers are carried in short spikes, not singly as in some other speedwells.

4 Coltsfoot flowers appear early in spring. Look for their thick, scaly stems. The leaves do not appear until the flowers have withered and died.

5 Cowslips are grassland plants which thrive on some grassy roadsides.

6 Butterbur grows on damp ground and is especially common on river banks. The flowers appear early in spring and attract lots of bees. The leaves appear later and may reach a metre across.

7 Greater stitchwort grows abundantly in many older hedgerows, especially on heavy clay soils. Each petal has a deep split down the middle.

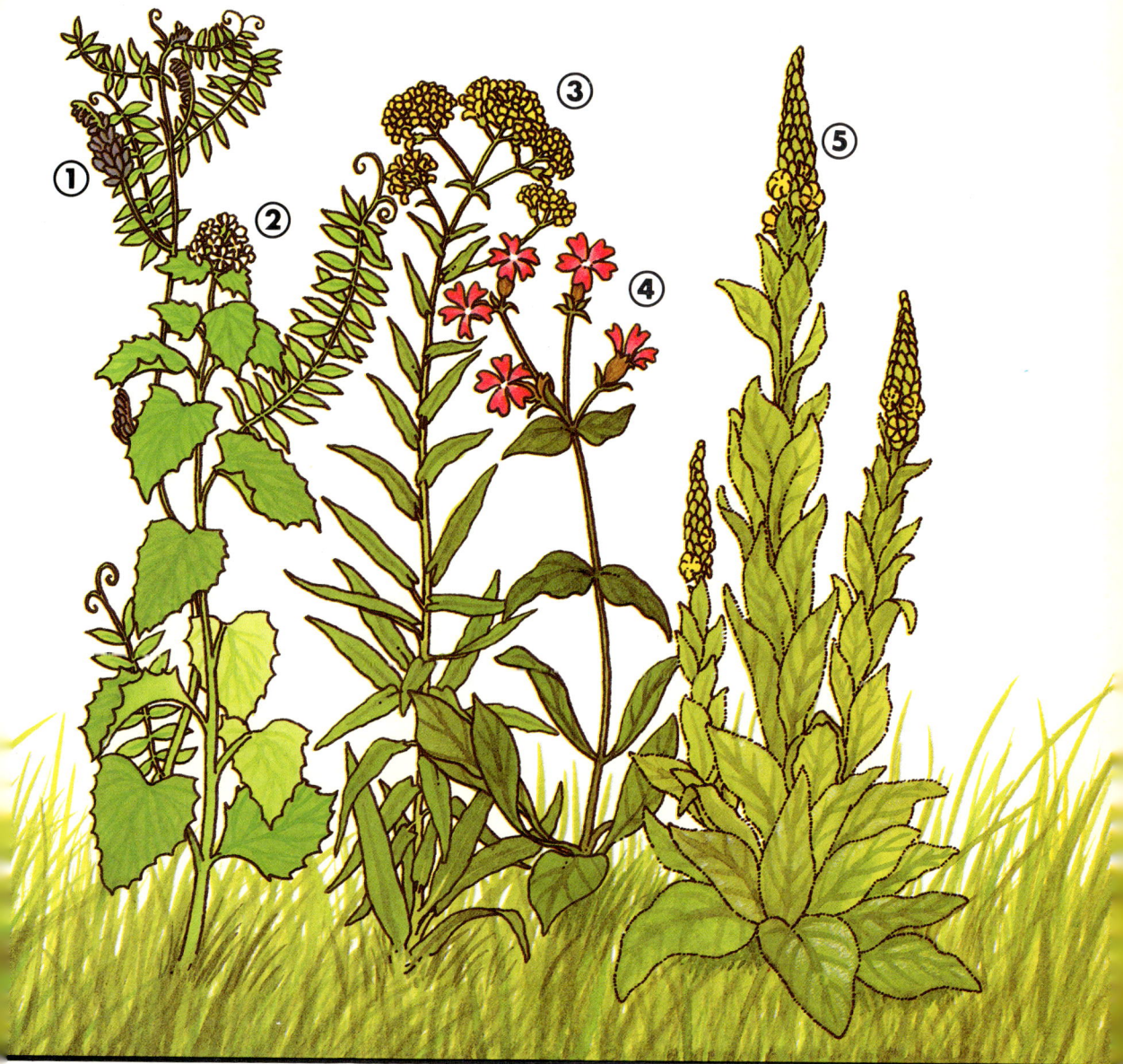

1 Tufted vetch climbs over other plants in the lower parts of the hedge by curling its tendrils around the other stems. You can see the tendrils at the tips of the leaves. Each leaf consists of up to 24 small leaflets.

2 Garlic mustard, also called Jack-by-the-Hedge, flowers in spring and summer. It often forms thick clumps in the hedge. Crush one of the leaves and smell it: can you smell the garlic scent?

3 Woad turns many dry roadsides bright yellow in spring and summer. In autumn the plants are covered with hanging black or dark brown fruits. The plant is rare in Britain but very common in southern Europe.

4 Red campion can be seen in flower for most of the year, but is at its best in late spring. There is also a white campion. The two often interbreed, producing plants with pale pink flowers.

5 Great mullein grows on dry verges and banks, especially where the soil has been disturbed and is not too grassy. Feel its soft, woolly leaves – they are covered in tiny white hairs. There are several other kinds of mullein without hairy leaves. Most have yellow flowers.

The thieving magpie

The magpie is surely one of the easiest birds to recognise. Whether it's hopping along the roadside or flying over the fields, you can always tell it by its black and white feathers and its very long tail. Try to get close to a magpie in bright sunshine. You will see that it is not strictly black and white – its glossy black feathers glint purple and green when the sun hits them.

Magpies eat almost anything, and pick up most of their food from the ground. Look for them hunting on the roadside verge. Notice how they often hop sideways, using their long tails to help them balance. Magpies eat grain and other fruits and seeds, but most of their meals are made up of animal matter. Snails, beetles and caterpillars are all eagerly snapped up, and these extraordinary birds will even ride on sheep's backs to look for flies and ticks in the wool. Watch out for this strange behaviour if you ever see magpies in the fields. Voles and other small animals are also caught and eaten by magpies, and the birds are happy to feast on dead animals as well. They also regularly raid other birds' nests and steal the eggs and young nestlings. In fact, magpies will steal practically anything they can pick up, especially if it is brightly coloured or shiny. This is why many magpie nests contain milk bottle tops, and even pieces of jewellery!

Magpies like to nest in tall, overgrown hedges. They make large, untidy nests – complete with roofs – of twigs cemented together with mud. The bird's long tail is very useful at times like these since it helps its owner to balance on the slender branches while the nest is being built. Try to find out what it does with its tail when actually inside the nest.

nature detective

More black-and-white birds

Keep your eyes open for these two other black and white birds when exploring the hedgerows. Both have relatively long tails but are much smaller than the magpie. Can you see any other differences? Look at their heads. Pied wagtails occur all over Europe in summer, but leave the northern parts for the winter because they cannot find enough insects to eat. The great grey shrike lives in most parts of Europe but only visits Britain in the winter. It eats insects, lizards and even small mammals. In flight it looks entirely black and white.

Look for the **pied wagtail** *(below)* around farms and villages, especially near water. Watch how it wags its tail while standing or strutting around. It catches insects on or near the ground. Its throat is largely white in winter.

The **great grey shrike** *(below)* usually sits on a prominent perch and keeps a sharp look out for its prey of large moths and lizards. It is often called the butcher bird because it hangs its victims on thorns until it's ready to eat.

Picture index

Alexander's 35
American mink 13
Argiope **spider** 32, 33

Bank vole 4, 20, 21
Bee
   leaf-cutter 19

   potter 8, 9
Beetle
   Cerambyx cerdo 14
   cockchafer 14
   stag 15
   tanner 14
Bindweed 4, 17, 25
Bittersweet 16, 25
Blackberry 21, 25
Blackbird 24
Blackthorn 24, 28
Blue tit 25
Bramble 5, 16, 24, 25
Brimstone butterfly 25, 26
Bryony 25
Bufftip moth caterpillar 23
Bullfinch 11
Butterbur 38
Butterfly
   brimstone 25, 26
   comma 26
   hedge brown 27
   holly blue 26

   map 26
   orange-tip 27

   ringlet 27
   small tortoiseshell 24
   wall 36

Caterpillar
   bufftip moth 23
   garden tiger moth 22
   gold-tail moth 31
   grey dagger moth 23
   magpie moth 22
   privet hawkmoth 22
   vapourer moth 31
Cerambyx cerdo 14
Chaffinch 11
Cleavers 17
Cockchafer 14

Coltsfoot 38
Comma butterfly 26
Cow parsley 35
Cowslip 4, 38
Cuckoo 5, 30, 31

Dance-fly 35
Dandelion 5, 24
Deadnettle
   red 8
   white 8, 24
Dogwood 28
Dunnock 5, 10, 25, 30

Elder 28
Emperor moth 23
English elm 29

Ferret 13
Fieldfare 24

Firecrest 6

Fool's parsley 35

Gall wasp 19
Garden tiger moth caterpillar 22
Garlic mustard 39
Germander speedwell 4, 38
Goldcrest 6
Goldfinch 10, 25
Gold-tail moth caterpillar 31
Greater stitchwort 38
Great grey shrike 41
Great mullein 39
Greenbottle 17

Greenfinch 10
Grey dagger moth caterpillar 23
Guelder rose 5

Hawthorn 24, 29
Hedge bindweed 4, 17, 25
Hedge brown butterfly 27
Hedgehog 25
Hedge woundwort 8
Hemlock 35
Henbit 8

Hogweed 25, 34, 35
Holly blue butterfly 26
Honeysuckle 5, 25
Hypogymnia physodes 37

Ivy 4, 16, 17
Ivy-leaved toadflax 38

Knapweed 25

Leaf-cutter bee 19
Lecanora muralis 37
Lesser celandine 24
Lichen
   Hypogymnia physodes 37
   Lecanora muralis 37
   Ochrolechia parella 37
   pixie-cup 37

   tree-lungwort 37
   Xanthoria 36
Little owl 11
Long-tailed tit 11

Magpie 4, 40, 41
Magpie moth caterpillar 22
Map butterfly 26
Millipede 36, 37
Mink 13

Ochrolechia parella 37
Orange-tip butterfly 27

Parsley
   cow 35
   fool's 35
Pied wagtail 41
Pincushion gall 18, 19
Pixie-cup lichen 37
Plantain 25
Polecat 13

Potter bee 8, 9

Privet hawkmoth caterpillar 22
Pussy willow 29

Rabbit 24
Red campion 39
Red deadnettle 8
Ringlet butterfly 27
Robin 19, 24
Robin's pincushion 18
Rose-slug 19

Sedge warbler 11
Self-heal 9
Shrew 20, 21
Small tortoiseshell butterfly 24
Snowberry 29
Spider
   Argiope 32, 33
   web 33
   zebra 37
Spindle 29
Stag beetle 15
Stinging nettle 4, 9
Stoat 12

Tanner beetle 14
Tit
   blue 25
Tree-lungwort 37
Tufted vetch 39
Turtle dove 10

Vapourer moth caterpillar 31
Violets 24

Wall butterfly 36
Wayfaring tree 28
Weasel 4, 13
White deadnettle 8, 24
Whitethroat 11
Wild privet 29
Wild rose 18, 19, 25
   hips 19, 24, 25
Wild snapdragon 38
Woad 39
Wren 7

Xanthoria 36

Yellow archangel 9
Yellowhammer 25

Zebra spider 37

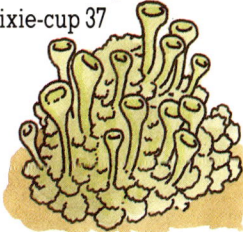

Panel index

A cuckoo's hairy dinner 31
An assortment of webs 32
Clinging cleavers 17
Deadnettle look-alikes 8
Eaters eaten 34
Gather the galls 19
How clean is your town? 37
How old is that hedge? 5
Keeping caterpillars 23
Look for the cuckoo 31
Looking for lichens 36
More big beetles 14
More black-and-white birds 40
More small birds 6
Stoat look-alikes 12
Teeth for the job 20
The hogweed's family 35
The ivy's feast 17
The rose's other guests 19
The stinging nettle's sting 9
Weavers at work 33